Bottom Rail on Top

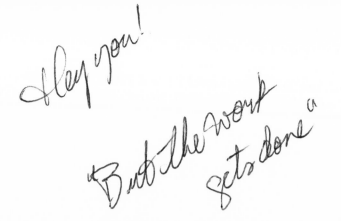

Hey you!
"But the work gets done"

Bottom Rail on Top
D.M. Bradford

BRICK BOOKS

Library and Archives Canada Cataloguing in Publication

Title: Bottom rail on top / D.M. Bradford.
Names: Bradford, D. M., author.
Description: Poems. | Includes bibliographical references.
Identifiers: Canadiana (print) 20230464645 | Canadiana (ebook) 20230464653 | ISBN
9781771316101 (softcover) | ISBN 9781771316125 (PDF) | ISBN 9781771316118 (EPUB)
Classification: LCC PS8603.R32855 B68 2023 | DDC C811/.6—dc23

We gratefully acknowledge the Canada Council for the Arts, the Government of Canada through the
Canada Book Fund, and the Ontario Arts Council for their support of our publishing program.

 Canada Council   Conseil des arts
for the Arts   du Canada

 ONTARIO ARTS COUNCIL
CONSEIL DES ARTS DE L'ONTARIO
an Ontario government agency
un organisme du gouvernement de l'Ontario

 Government   Gouvernement
of Canada   du Canada

Edited by Cecily Nicholson.

Cover image:
Hugo McCloud
consumption stacks - pink, 2018
plastic merchandise bags mounted on panel
77 1/4 x 67 1/4 inches (196.2 x 170.8 cm)
© Hugo McCloud
Courtesy: Sean Kelly

Author photo by Annie France Noël.
The book is set in Adobe Garamond Pro and Optima.
Design by Emma Allain.
Printed and bound by Coach House Printing.

Brick Books
487 King St. W.
Kingston, ON
K7L 2X7   **BRICK BOOKS**
www.brickbooks.ca

Though much of the work of Brick Books takes place on the ancestral lands of the Anishinaabeg,
Haudenosaunee, Huron-Wendat, and Mississaugas of the Credit peoples, our editors, authors, and
readers from many backgrounds are situated from coast to coast to coast in Canada on the traditional
and unceded territories of over six hundred nations who have cared for Turtle Island from time
immemorial. While living and working on these lands, we are committed to hearing and returning
the rightful imaginative space to the poetries, songs, and stories that have been untold, under-told,
wrongly told, and suppressed through colonization.

Table of Contents

It is a condition I will never know because English is not my mother tongue. It is my father tongue and one which meant me and my mother no good. But it is my mother tongue and father tongue all wrapped together in some kind of ghastly embrace—or is it struggle? Or perhaps both?

M. NourbeSe Philip

Don't let us lack the heart-catching, odd beauty, the nourishing heartbreak, of "The Idea of Ancestry."

Gwendolyn Brooks

"The story of the escaped slave, who joins the Union Army, encounters his master and says, 'Howdy Massa. Bottom rail on top, this time' is such a lovely end. More coming. I'm working now."

Ta-Nehisi Coates, The Atlantic, 2009

Leads to:

"In 1865 a black soldier who recognized his former master among a group of Confederate prisoners he was guarding called out a greeting: 'Hello, massa; bottom rail on top dis time!' Would this new arrangement of rails last?"

James M. McPherson, Battle Cry of Freedom, 1988

Leads to:

"Recognizing his former master among the prisoners he was guarding, a black soldier greeted him effusively, 'Hello, massa; bottom rail top dis time!'"

Leon F. Litwack, Been in the Storm So Long, 1979

Leads to:

"The command was sent as prisoners to Ship Island, which is nothing but a bleak sand-bar, without any shade or shelter upon it of any kind, and kept there in the hot sun, guarded in a very brutal manner by negroes, for twenty days [...] One of the negroes, who ordered the boys about and guarded them, often accosted them with the expression or something similar, 'who be you rebels now? bottom rail on top dis time sure.'"

Ephraim McDowell Anderson, Memoirs: Historical and Personal, 1868

Leads to:

rope to

Not a poem

but fatherlands so far gone
    barely dawned
way down on all them

all whites on the big-house tour

Not a poem

but plantation dining room
    ceiling pulley fan
boy fatherlands and rope

Not a poem

but brick kiln children
    firing fatherlands
morning cure and smote

Not a poem

but that 28 oaks alley
      fatherlands limbs pretty
still hanging
      heavy low

and not another of

      on the grounds
not serving brunch

"dine. sleep. explore."
vacherie, louisiana

Not a poem, but a big house is a big house. Imagine I'm standing in one being told every brick that makes it up was made on site by children. That said children didn't not look like me, and kept the fire going around the clock. Imagine the tour guide announcing all this, dressed to look like the mistress of the house. Someone helps dress her in the morning, pile the whole thing on, button it up the back. Or there's well-placed Velcro and she does it on her own. Either way, imagine there's a sound just outside the window, a clinking like bricks, and she imagines children stacking them. And then every day she talks about the bricks. Every day she impresses it upon us that the walls are three bricks thick. Every day I'm out here I'm wearing selvedge denim, Horween leather boots, cotton tops from unknown places. And every day since I stay impressed because here are the details. Here she is pointing her ruffled sleeve at the enslaver's will's list of properties, whatever you call such a thing. Here it says: Four-poster mahogany bedframe, $30. Here it says: Déterville, 34 years old, $1200. Here everything was made by the enslaved, and so here everything made is worthless. Apart from the means to make them. Here Meanna, "Mulatto seamstress," and her two boys and three girls were worth two-and-half times as much as the fifteen cart horses, worth fifty-odd beds. The things remain, the people don't. I pout my way through the gift shop. I wish I knew what I ordered for lunch. I wonder how many folks around Vacherie know about the name of their town. I assume there were cows down here. But for those of us who speak the language now, the first thing Vacherie brings to mind is a gratuitously crappy thing. Like a pile of shit out by the levee. It gives cows a bad name.

ashes to

Not a poem

but a turtle back off monkland
    river just about hid
the island frosted
now and again

what I might scrub
    can to can't
see right off myself

Not a poem

but my wintering and ash
    my shed and vanity alight
never soft spoken

Not a poem

but my liberté cottage cheese tub
    of viva cold pressed coconut
and fine lantic silk
my ass smelling like a fish

Not a poem

but takes leave of my flake
   granulated clean
scaled on the cheap
from across a whole ocean

Not a poem

but what a simple treat
    what softly remains
my merest skin

Not a poem

but non-hydrogenated
    the best part of waking
up click click

stock

Not a poem

but then I read
into the incidents

Not a poem

but fatherlands likened a dog people
grecian-named levee spaniels
    first boughs
and then wrists

**"so that their toes barely
touched the ground…" s graham**

Not a poem

but the seven years restock

"current in georgia and all
the more commercial parts"

Not a poem

but floggings by the hymn

Not a poem

but ten thousand angels
how can die boys
    how growing house girls
in waiting

Not a poem

but gone before the king

**"the affinities of pleasure
and mortification..."** s hartman

Not a poem

but in the family stable
how dr breedwads
    or husbandry

how missouri v celia
    alfred v state

"the vested rights of others"
"the very act of shame"

Not a poem

but how fatherlands the livestock
beds the wash hog
    muddies the kinder bellies
by the bellyful bines

no sun at all
up for the taking

"the south's prettiest small town"

Not a poem but a succession of little cuts. You hear about Sally Hemings over and over again. You don't hear that much about Martha Jefferson, Thomas Jefferson's first wife, being Sally's half-sister. You don't hear much about Betty Hemings, Martha's father's enslaved mistress, Sally's mother. You don't hear much about the other half-siblings, how many of them Martha, along with Thomas, inherited, the Hemings family among 135. Commonplace horrors. Allegedly Martha was dead by the time Thomas started going after Sally, which is when the story most often told really begins. And it often begins as a story of love, and/or resilience, and/or heritage, or as an expansively colourful footnote to the legacy of a complicated foundational genius of the many-foundered nation. Not often a story of no consent or right given. Or of an historic practitioner of an historical practice. What Thomas might have chalked up to his hands-on approach to what he might have called curational enslavement. Another thing about Thomas not so much unusual, for the time, as unusually resourced. Because there it all goes on the "How African-American Cuisine Transformed America" Netflix show: the immaculately conserved, still operational, as-it-was kitchen at Thomas's Monticello. A setting for the telling of the story of his enslaved cook—Sally's older brother James, Martha's half-brother—trained in France to cook like a Frenchman. Because, as the show insists on highlighting, one place all that rape went down: also the birthplace of mac and cheese. Wrought in the birthplace of so many things. Imagine that. High on the hog for a moment, Black cuisine serves the cravings of Black excellence. The father of mac and cheese. And its aunt. Imagine that. Right there with the foundation, blood quantum, covetous math.

tempur

Not a poem

but I did my rump good
broken even

Not a poem

but made my shift
    a slow and crawly

Not a poem

but of shaking hands
   worked my deep coral
my lavendered disc jelly

Not a poem

but my crust degenerative
    years long mustered seven
I learnt sets and waited

short of breaking even
    the one part of me
off to soften into this
ikea topper unit

Not a poem

but now this new flowery
    medicated mattress

Not a poem

but this dauphin pressure pointless
    memory tundra fresh
bed of latex lettuce

Not a poem

but 1500 and smart wick
    myrcene and my vitamix
purple and my feat
tinctured and pumiced

I can't wait
    to just dream

of the gross cost
of my sleep

loophole

Not a poem

but alive still

"if we think of the 'flesh'
as a primary narrative..." h spillers

Not a poem

but don't get lost
pled and poured over
    ain't I's as the hold
and still

"dat's it, honey" f gage, 1863
"despite my fantasies of flight" f wilderson
"between-a hawk and a buzzard" m robinson, 1851

Not a poem

but garret the breastwork
   sojourn the bulwarks
gin a cotton fatherlands prying in
and still

"...seared, divided, ripped-apartness, riveted to" spillers
   "an in-between location" ma green-barteet

Not a poem

but harriet writing about linda
     in the shed's crawlspace
listening for her kids

"and oh, christian mothers!" 1853
"my own way to obtain it" 155

Not a poem

but who writing her seven years
sowed by shingle light
　　one hole by gimlet
two little faces floating in

"neither the brain or talent to write it" 1853
"it put a lucky thought into my head" 129

Not a poem

but cunning versus cunning

"as good as comedy to me" 145

Not a poem

but notes for the flinting
nook scrawled in reps

"made to render them a service" 142
"defeat the object that I wish to pursue" 1853

Not a poem

but patient in tribulation
    fervent in spirit

mount auburn cemetery, cambridge, mass.
"where no eye but god's could see me" 148

Not a poem

but serving the lord
none but the one
    writ fatherlands croak
out aunt martha's attic

"what made me think it was you" 173
"and the omission of one or two passages. —ed." 1853

Not a poem

but till the cut breaks
        wrote with a prayer
lead out of the darkness

wrote faint of body
        strong of purpose

"an assurance of repetition" ja snead
"whispered through a crack" 161

Not a poem

but to write at last
        past the old place
one last time

by boat
the breeze and the sunshine
        north by fatherlands
ten days and ten nights

"territory that defies all laws" 177
"she has not told the half" 1853

Not a poem but the problem of proneness. Not the aftermath of her proneness, of Harriet's forever messed-up body carrying those cramped years of hiding in the family garret, hiding from Dr. enslavement. Not the problem of its likeliness either, of Harriet Beecher Stowe, for one, who wouldn't believe any of her story at first, and asked her northerly employer, of all people, to confirm it—the story she wasn't liable to start writing till her grandmother Molly, her story's Aunt Martha, passed back in Everton. But I mean the problem of the story some of us have tried to figure that crawlspace is: the scrawl in her head, the desperate quiet to keep up, the whatever's between them. The whole while not just bearing fruit and subterfuge one letter at a time. Not just the mess of covert exercises taking her frame to the future, in a little sail ship, headed north, back together, planning forever, dear readership. Not just prone as I am writing this. Not just the irony of writing her mouth shut. Not just the telling fact of that other Harriet's refusal to write the book's foreword. But the lot of those inclined to imagine her years in hiding as prone as Winslow Homer's *The Gulf Stream* maroon. Her toes tucked up on a drifting bit of boat wood, sharks circling as thick as the water. Before they imagine her after, prone as Kerry James Marshall's *Gulf Stream* weekender sailors, given to leisure, almost whimsical, loaded and well. When she's really only as prone as if she's at once the maroon and the sailors, and she's also Marshall and Homer, and she's also more work to come. She's also the sun coming up. She's also watching it come up. Writes it down on free soil. I'm unsure how she enjoys the work. But the work gets done.

overseeroverseer

Not a poem

but a likkle truth
   the sound of the beast
tells me it's no
good resisting

the -woop itself
   gone off at
the doorlatch's click

Not a poem

but charters the beast
    shinier than the lake
louder than the change
room -woop wide
    as the whole bay

yonge and deploying
    the second it clicks
the -woop declares me
be stilled where I stand

Not a poem

but flanking my thick
    fuddling trunk broadened
as the three mirrors reflect

that the -woop will
    keep remaining
even as I will not

Not a poem

but even as I vacate
    its foreshortened levi's I don't
and do want

Not a poem

but even down
seven allusive flights

even as the -woop stops
    the second I walk
thru the exit

even as I feel sick
    and then I am

Not a poem

but a sale is a sale

I'm back for a couch
    the very same
weekend

"a loud noise in the heavens"

Not a poem

but word about stono
lukango and jemmy

"as fully and amply as if
such rebellious negroes had undergone
a formal trial and condemnation" 1740

Not a poem

but word about caesar
and prince and cuffee
and fort george
ye happy spirits
to the ground in nyc

"corner of liberty and trinity" 1741

Not a poem

but word of gabriel's
    richmond death or liberty
gallowed by pharoah
washed by the storming

"worth about $9,000 or so" 1800

Not a poem

but word of deslondes and andry
    the german coast three hundred storied
strong and yet

"like crows sitting on long poles" 1811

Not a poem

but the word about southampton

lilies nat's new songs field
    calls to live or fatherlands by

"on the appearance of the sign" 1831

Not a poem

but about the hundreds
    fatherlands put down
heads
mounted like signs

"blackhead signpost rd"
"negro head rd"

71

Not a poem

but stuck up along the road
    for the rise
done felled at least 51
not poor whites

and children on both sides

"thought no better of themselves
than they did of" 1831

Not a poem but, like a poet's poet, a deterrent's deterrent. I had a dream that woke me up at dawn convinced I had forgotten about all these other Blackhead Signpost Roads all over the place. I woke up meaning to list them here, to dapple the map with them. As if there's a Blackhead Signpost Road through Greene. Or the one just outside Wilmington. Former Jerusalem. Dead centre of town. Right into Courtland. An unmissable thing. Along the poor side of the lake. But really it's just the one, technically. Shortened to Signpost Road a couple of years ago, but the full name's still there when you google. And really it's way too much if you go looking for the others. It's the maybe twenty-three heads, for a start, not notable enough for their own street in New Orleans. Is that better or worse? It's the nearly hundred heads along River Road, parish law, it bears repeating, like crows on long poles. Common enough a warning, the idea gets tired as the afternoon wears on. All over again, the idea works over sandy loam, kitchen intel, cut harvest, mobile holdings, short staple. The idea counts the hundred and twenty or so Black people killed in the aftermath of that one solar eclipse in Southampton, and this time the idea counts probably just the one head. Counts a blacksmith to mark the crossroads of the rebellion. Maybe named Alfred. Maybe not much part of the rebellion at all. We don't know now. But they painted the pole black after the head decayed. Blackhead Signpost. And when the emergency response system came along, they gave the road its name. And generations of people travelled that same road with that same name for decades.

deus hose

Not a poem

but my studious pain is
so dark and romantic

Not a poem

but so hot and angelic

taking me out on the town
    in my tasmanian teal
down endowment

my very own patagonian fill
    is the absolute warmest
kindling of guilt

Not a poem

but o so loftily
   what I might live
a long time while pretty
ashamed and jobless

Not a poem

but passing more roughage
than a water closet

and this holey commode
    that still don't fray
calls the buildup architectonic
calls this strain a shift

Not a poem

but a savour and severance
   I might never be
done fucking with

parch to the sea

Not a poem

but is god dead

moses's by her winter fatherlands
    rooted here

gone catchall lake providence

"all the uptowns you never
been to but read about
and have some cousins in" f moten
"can't pull us up" 1859

Not a poem

but catchall frontline jacobs
   fatherlands dispatches
born at railroad speed

"let me tell you of another place...
little one-day freeman" 1862

Not a poem

but fatherlands by errancy
    monroes by the plum street
bodies by the mule pen
by grants to be free

of being freed
    by contraband

"the (fort) monroe doctrine" 1861
"in obedience to some common order" col dickson
"with such an army of them..." maj gen grant, 1862

Not a poem

but for the cannons

Not a poem

but about css planter by pioneer
    corps by foot and fodder
spangled to the fatherlands
uphill at nashville

"a very intelligent contraband" cmdr parrott
"with the greatest promptitude and gallantry" maj gen rosecrans, 1863
"presented by the colored ladies of murfreesboro"
december 16, 1864

Not a poem

but upon the tempest
    by pillow and earthen
by fort wagner fatherlands
and o like men

boys the old flag
    never touched the ground

"remember fort pillow!"
"in which he was twice severely wounded"
july 18, 1863

Not a poem

but by fatherlands onward
    by sherman's column
davis's cut loose bridge

and ebenezer swollen
by creek drowned hangers on
    killed or caught
by the hundreds

by the not ever migrations

december 9, 1864
"no writer who was not upon the ground
can gloss the matter over for me" col kerr

Not a poem but 0.2% of total Southern land. Subject to the premise of tracts from the Saint Johns River up to the Charleston Islands. To be confiscated, "for the settlement of the BLACKS now made free," by William Tecumseh Sherman's Special Order No. 15, approved by Abraham Lincoln. A few months before the assassination. And followed by Andrew Johnson and expedient oaths and amnesty and land restoration. Followed by the Black Codes, preventing Black land ownership, the painstaking criteria for "officially confiscated," and leasing schemes to handle the rest. Forty acres and a mule, a maybe seven-month-long assurance. Born and dead in 1865. Ebenezer Creek, hundreds of Black people drowned, literally cut off by the Union from any and all means to get to freedom: one among a number of recorded incidents, amidst notably solemn something-has-to-be-done's, that influenced the short-lived Freedmen's Bureau promise. There are people alive and well now who wonder aloud if the land would have made a difference. As land did in the Cherokee Nation. Cherokee Freedmen made full Cherokee citizens. Cherokee Freedmen free to claim and use Cherokee land in the public domain, whether an acre or four hundred. Usufructuary rights, no Bureau, so they built their own schools. No decommissioned Union mules, so Zack Foreman Sr. turned a single, sickly, abandoned cow into a four-hundred-head herd. And soon, the town of Foreman. Mattie Foreman, a schoolteacher, allegedly its first postmistress. Son Roscoe succeeding her in 1914. Zack Jr., a Langston University graduate, a well-known Monarch in the Negro League. Cousin Hooks a catcher for the All Nations. And another son, one that didn't quite make it, named W.T. Sherman Foreman. Every August 4th the town would hold an Emancipation Proclamation picnic, with Zack Sr. and Mattie as its king and queen. The Curtis Act took a lot of their land away, same as other Cherokee Nation citizens. But Sheridan, Roscoe, Zack Jr., Dewey, Rhoda, Urah, and Mattie's inherited estate at the time of Zack Sr.'s passing on August 5th, 1916: still seven times the median of Black wealth today. I wish I knew that first cow's name.

run

Not a poem

and yet the good goddess
of victory cuts MAX
    wants my cut FLEX
my cut EPIC momentous
    shod of a habit

Not a poem

yet wants it cut FREE
wants my RN cut ODYSSEY
	cut REACT wants
my cut ZOOM clip
	my SHIELD cut remedy

full blooded and cut LEGEND
frolic cut FLYKNIT
	OFF-NOIR cut SUMMIT
gainful as my raw cut
	LIME BLAST gait

Not a poem

yet wants my cut ULTRA
my tight VAPOR cut
    PHANTOM king dri-FIT
every DARK CITRON stride

Not a poem

yet reveals my cut RISE
cut AIR whole ponied
    in my cut TURBO all
black Pegasus 35s

to be seen cut FLY
at home SIZE MY SWOOSH
    a few feet outside

every step of me JUST
    DO IT the bits
leave behind

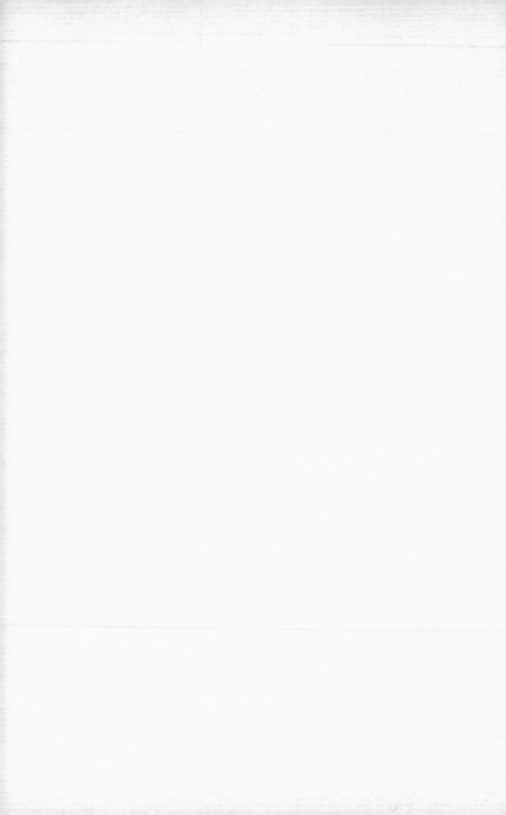

new corps

Not a poem

but given a uniform

"i observed a very remarkable trait about them" gen butler

Not a poem

but give 'em fatherlands US a brass
number 'em an eagle
    button 'em what a bullet pocketful
of 'em can earn

set forth from the hand
first under fire

"woe betide us if we fail to embrace it..." f douglass
"but as the plank to the ship"

Not a poem

but the heaviest blow
    at last in blue coats
under good white officers

"and to aid in capturing more" gen grant, august 23, 1863

Not a poem

but the pontoon corps
d'afrique fatherlands guard
    dark and thorny
poised and butchered
    out of port hudson

given a new age coffle's
    bargain and garrison

"ferro iis libertas perveniet"
"(immense cheering)" july 6, 1863

101

Not a poem, but if better soldiers never shouldered a musket. And if freedom. If theirs by the sword. And patience. If by a common origin. Tardy. A common language. Cold. If a common literature. Dull. A common glory. Indifferent. Mysterious properties. Seems it only took a thousand or so Black soldiers to truly convince Benjamin Butler. I wonder what Frederick Douglass might have thought of that. At times convinced, as I'm sure he seemed aloud, that Black soldiers would get to the same pay. That they'd get more than a few of their own commissions. That this was how they'd die or come home undeniable citizens. Amended without exclusion. Deep in the course of ages. In the solemn shades, the silent continents. If *in a dance of blood*—I mean, the sheer turns of phrase the man would draw out for those who showed up to hear. And in the most distressing colors. If the prostrate form, the uncovered head, the cringing attitude, the bated breath. Swift and zealous. If fitted through their sentences. Radical and determined. Though if duly convicted. If the din of business. And peace among them. The whites. Never lacked for a tongue. If the withered branch, and the unsightly rock. If a mere speck in the life of a nation. Disastrous times. If had cheap. Presenting the semblance of paradise.

lil chug

Not a poem

tho when we come up
    on the cyclical impasse
back underground at old mill

Not a poem

tho when petey and his peak wicker
    ensemble insist on making ours
an intimate seating arrangement

when they twang up the whole
    breadth of the subway car's
dispersing not-me audience

Not a poem

tho when they don't lose it
    as much as loose
their good private shit

breaknecking their way
    to what might be
the right kind of station

tangentially at a loss and circling
    in and staring me down
and received and open

to not stopping at all

Not a poem

tho when I nod my fucking head
    till they get off at islington

when I keep their mouths going
    and they transfer with me
up on the airport rocket

and we take it to the bridge
    baby turn our shit to change
on my last sweet token

Not a poem

tho when I forget everything they said
   I keep the one secret
growing so good and big

   I pray to quote myself on it

"dis time"

Not a poem

but given old masters
down the river
    fenced in

"nothing but a bleak sand-bar..." 1868

Not a poem

but given dragooned
    old boys
beneath the negro's heel

"oh, shame! where is thy blush?"

Not a poem

but given a bit of white meat
    and one fatherlands
heard tell of it

"for no offence at all
that any one could discover"

Not a poem

but that ain't shit now
    massa lockdown given hell
of an uppity fatherlands bidness

or given whatever
    white lie of it

"let my people go!" 1886

Not a poem

but the way the times
    have found us equal
companions in death

"until we, today, have
done our part fighting it" 1987

Not a poem

but given the storm so long
    chalked up to pbs

sweet to greet the old fatherland
    shackled with the rest

at last and yet

**"more from the ken burns
in the classroom collection"**
"oh lord, give me more time to pray"

Not a poem

but the bottom rail on top
    movin' on up
and still the same old fence

"all the evils of that evil day" 1901

Not a poem

but young gifted fatherlands and
    no reruns brother and
let my people
living just enough
    the same fucking again

Not a poem

but when you come home
    say it loud I'm
but a train a-comin'
endless days
    and just like a river I've

"lord, i feel like running"

Not a poem

but I'm close to the edge

Not a poem

and when it hit
    you feel no pain

"lord, and never get tired (oh yes)"

Not a poem

you don't need no baggage

Not a poem

streets of gold

"(thank you, thank you)"

Not a poem

unless

Bibliography

I've tried to make this record of my cited, rendered and consulted works and sources an exhaustive one. *Bottom Rail on Top* makes heavy use of archival and critical materials: there's where I found those bits and pieces, and there's the experience, textures, turns, and problems of having found them. There's documenting where I got all this stuff, and there's the hand in marking it out, in scoring and stitching it together.

With that in mind, there are a few maybe fun, maybe frustrating decisions on my part I'd like to acknowledge. The ways these materials are used in the work represent my attempt to render the fever and scrawl that goes into sleuthing out and making sense of the historicizations they represent, and to incite a reader's own feel for those motions. To that effect, the tracks and field notes I've left for readers and myself in the subterrain of each page are intentionally informal in their notational style.

In each case, I tried to give the date, page number, name, place or mix of the above that felt the most urgent and necessary to me, and which enabled the source and line of inquiry the note marks to be searched and found online. Sometimes no extra context was given—if the source is the same as the previous note, for instance, or if attribution is not needed or appropriate.

The hope is you've at times enjoyed picking up the trail. If that wasn't the adventure to choose for yourself, maybe next time. Whichever way, I completely understand.

American Battlefield Trust. "Fort Wagner," American Battlefield Trust, 2018. https://www.battlefields.org/learn/civil-war/battles/fort-wagner.

Anderson, Ephraim McD. *Memoirs: Historical and Personal; Including the Campaigns of the First Missouri Confederate Brigade.* St. Louis: Times Printing, 1868.

Ashwill, Gary. "Not All Ball Players Are Broke: Zack Foreman of the Kansas City Monarchs," Agate Type, September 25, 2011. https://agatetype.typepad.com/agate_type/zack-foreman/.

Beard, Rick. "Forty Acres and a Mule," *Opinionator* (blog), *New York Times*, January 16, 2015. https://archive.nytimes.com/opinionator.blogs.nytimes.com/2015/01/16/forty-acres-and-a-mule/.

Bickham, William D. *Rosecrans' Campaign with the Fourteenth Army Corps, Or the Army of the Cumberland: A Narrative of Personal Observations, with an Appendix, Consisting of Official Reports of the Battle of Stone River.* Cincinnati: Moore, Wilstach, Keys, 1863.

Biggs, Greg. "The Battle of Nashville," American Battlefield Trust, 2014. https://www.battlefields.org/learn/articles/battle-nashville.

Bradford, Sarah H. *Harriet, the Moses of Her People.* New York: Geo. R. Lockwood & Son, 1886.

Brophy, Alfred. "Blackhead Signpost Road Needs Another Sign," *Tidewater News*, August 15, 2015. https://www.thetidewaternews.com/2015/08/15/blackhead-signpost-road-needs-another-sign/.

Brown, James. "Say It Loud–I'm Black and I'm Proud." *A Soulful Christmas.* King Records, 1968.

Burns, Ken. "The Civil War: Bottom Rail on Top," PBS, 2015. Accessed via US proxy. https://www.pbs.org/video/civil-war-bottom-rail-top/#:~:text=Clip%3A%20Season%201%20%7C%207m%2049s.

Butler, Benjamin F. *Autobiography and Personal Reminiscences of Major-General Benj. F. Butler: Butler's Book*. Boston: A.M. Thayer, 1892.

Campbell, Annie. "Excerpts from South Carolina Slave Code of 1740 No. 670 (1740)." U.S. History Scene, July 14, 2015. https://ushistoryscene.com/article/excerpts-south-carolina-slave-code-1740-no-670-1740/.

Canadian Broadcasting Corporation. *Confederate Plaque on Hudson's Bay Store in Montreal*, August 17, 2017. Photograph. https://i.cbc.ca/1.4248235.1502821888!/fileImage/httpImage/jefferson-davis-plaque.jpg.

Clark, Peter H. *The Black Brigade of Cincinnati: Being a Report of Its Labors and a Muster-Roll of Its Members; Together with Various Orders, Speeches, etc., Relating to It*. Cincinnati: Joseph B. Boyd, 1864.

Coates, Ta-Nehisi. "Bottom Rail on Top," *Atlantic*, June 17, 2009. https://www.theatlantic.com/entertainment/archive/2009/06/bottom-rail-on-top/19547/.

Columbia University. "Hughson's Tavern," Mapping the African American Past. https://maap.columbia.edu/place/4.html.

Cooke, Sam. "A Change Is Gonna Come." *Ain't That Good News*. RCA, 1964.

Dead Prez. "Hip Hop." *Let's Get Free*. Loud Records, 2002.

Douglass, Frederick. "His Speech on the Color Question." Library of Congress, 1875. https://www.loc.gov/resource/mss11879.23001/?sp=2&r=-0.46.

Douglass, Frederick. *Great Speeches by Frederick Douglass*. Edited by James Daley. Mineola: Dover, 2013.

Douglass, Frederick, and James W Ford. *Negroes and the National War Effort*. New York: Workers Library Publishers, 1942.

Douglass, Frederick, and William L. Garrison. *Narrative of the Life of Frederick Douglass, an American Slave*. Boston: Anti-Slavery Office, 1849.

Dubois, Ja'net. "Movin' On Up." Theme from *The Jeffersons*. CBS, 1975.

Du Bois, W.E.B. "The Freedmen's Bureau," *Atlantic*, March 1, 1901. https://www.theatlantic.com/magazine/archive/1901/03/the-freedmens-bureau/308772/.

Duke Franklin Humanities Institute. "Left of Black | Black Women of the Southampton Slave Revolt with Vanessa M. Holden." YouTube, 2022. https://www.youtube.com/watch?v=VGeQWsKk0Hw&t=360s.

Explore Georgia. "March to the Sea: Ebenezer Creek Historical Marker," 2010. https://www.exploregeorgia.org/rincon/history-heritage/civil-war/march-to-the-sea-ebenezer-creek-historical-marker.

Fields, Barbara. "The Civil War; Interviews with Barbara Fields." By Ken Burns. *American Archive of Public Broadcasting*, 1987. https://americanarchive.org/catalog/cpb-aacip_509-2r3nv99t98.

The (Fort) Monroe Doctrine. 1861. Lithograph on wove paper. Library of Congress. https://www.loc.gov/pictures/resource/cph.3a36574/.

Franklin, Aretha. "Respect." *I Never Loved a Man the Way I Love You*. Atlantic Records, 1967.

Friends of Mount Auburn. "Harriet Jacobs, 1813–1897," Mount Auburn Cemetery, 2011. https://mountauburn.org/harriet-jacobs-1813-1897/.

Gates Jr., Henry Louis. "Did African-American Slaves Rebel? *The African Americans: Many Rivers to Cross*. PBS, 2013. https://www.pbs.org/wnet/african-americans-many-rivers-to-cross/history/did-african-american-slaves-rebel/.

Graham, Stephen. *The Soul of John Brown*. New York: MacMillan, 1920.

Grandmaster Flash and the Furious Five. "The Message." *The Message*. Sugar Hill Records, 1982.

Grant, Ulysses S. "Chapter 30." *Personal Memoirs of U.S. Grant*. New York: Charles L. Webster, 1885. Ebook.

Gray, Thomas R., Nat Turner, and Paul Royster (Depositor). "The Confessions of Nat Turner (1831)." *Electronic Texts in American Studies* 15. 1831.

Green-Barteet, Miranda A. "'The Loophole of Retreat': Interstitial Spaces in Harriet Jacobs's Incidents in the Life of a Slave Girl." *South Central Review* 30, no. 2 (2013): 53–72.

Hall, Donald, and Etheridge Knight. "Donald Hall and Etheridge Knight Reading Their Poems." Introduced by Gwendolyn Brooks. 1986. Audio, 35:08–35:18. Library of Congress. https://www.loc.gov/item/88740105/.

Harper's Weekly. "Heroism," June 7, 1862. http://www.sonofthesouth.net/leefoundation/civil-war/1862/june/louisiana-tigers.htm.

Hartman, Saidiya V. *Scenes of Subjection: Terror, Slavery, and Self-Making in Nineteenth-Century America.* New York: Oxford University Press, 1997.

Hickox, Will. "Remember Fort Pillow!" *Opinionator* (blog), New York Times, April 11, 2014. https://archive.nytimes.com/opinionator.blogs.nytimes.com/2014/04/11/remember-fort-pillow/.

Historical Society of the New York Courts. "Trials Relating to the New York Slave Insurrection, 1741," August 7, 2019. https://history.nycourts.gov/case/slave-conspiracy-trials.

Holden, Vanessa M. *Surviving Southampton: African American Women and Resistance in Nat Turner's Community.* Champaign: University of Illinois Press, 2021.

Homer, Winslow. *The Gulf Stream.* 1899. Oil on canvas. Metropolitan Museum of Art, New York. https://www.metmuseum.org/art/collection/search/11122.

Hutchins, Zachary. "Sojourner Truth: The Libyan Sibyl," Documenting the American South. University of North Carolina, 2008. https://docsouth.unc.edu/highlights/sojournertruth.html#:~:text=During%20the%20nineteenth%20century%2C%20Sojourner.

Hutchison, Michael, and Greg Timmons. "African-American Troops and Robert Gould Shaw of the 54th Massachusetts Regiment," Ken Burns in the Classroom: The Civil War. PBS LearningMedia, 2002. https://pbslearningmedia.org/resource/african-american-troops-lesson-plan/ken-burns-the-civil-war/kenburnsclassroom/.

The Impressions. "People Get Ready." *People Get Ready*. ABC-Paramount, 1965.

Jackson, Mahalia. "How I Got Over." *Sings the Best-Loved Hymns of Dr. Martin Luther King, Jr.* Columbia Records, 1968.

Jacobs, Harriet A. *Incidents in the Life of a Slave Girl: Written by Herself.* 1861. Reprint, New York: Penguin, 2000. Ebook.

Jacobs, Harriet A. (as A Fugitive Slave). "Letter from a Fugitive Slave," *New York Daily Tribune*, June 21, 1853. Documenting the American South. University of North Carolina. https://docsouth.unc.edu/fpn/jacobs/support16.html.

Jacobs, Harriet A. (as Linda). "Life among the Contrabands," *Liberator*, September 5, 1862. http://fair-use.org/the-liberator/1862/09/05/the-liberator-32-36.pdf.

KRS-One. *Sound of Da Police*. Jive Records, 1993.

Leavitt, Sarah. "Confederate Plaque on Montreal Hudson's Bay Store Removed," CBC, August 15, 2017. https://www.cbc.ca/news/canada/montreal/jefferson-davis-confederate-plaque-montreal-1.4248206.

The Liberator. "New England Convention of Colored Citizens," August 26, 1859. http://fair-use.org/the-liberator/1859/08/26/the-liberator-29-34.pdf.

Litwack, Leon F. *Been in the Storm so Long: The Aftermath of Slavery.* New York: Vintage, 1979. Ebook.

Lothrop, George E. *Boys the Old Flag Never Touched the Ground.* Sheet music. Duke University Digital Repository, 1909. https://repository.duke.edu/dc/hasm/a9088.

Marshall, Kerry James. *Gulf Stream*. 2003. Acrylic and glitter on canvas. Metropolitan Museum of Art, New York. https://www.metmuseum.org/art/collection/search/668369.

McPherson, James M. *Battle Cry of Freedom: The Civil War Era*. New York: Oxford University Press, 2003. Ebook.

Medal of Honor Convention. "William H. Carney." http://www.mohconvention.com/tn-recipient/108/william-h-carney/.

Miller, Melinda C. "Essays on Race and the Persistence of Economic Inequality." *Journal of Economic History* 70, no. 2 (2010): 468–72.

―――. "Cherokee Nation Policies After the Civil War Show That Reparations Work," *Washington Post*, May 24, 2021. https://www.washingtonpost.com/outlook/2021/05/24/cherokee-nation-policies-after-civil-war-show-that-reparations-work/.

Moten, Fred. "uc santa barbara and crenshaw follies." *The Service Porch*, 11–13. Seattle: Letter Machine Editions, 2016.

―――. "Knowledge of Freedom." *Stolen Life*, 1–95. Durham: Duke University Press, 2018.

National First Ladies' Library. "First Lady Biography: Martha Jefferson." http://archive.firstladies.org/biographies/firstladies.aspx?biography=3.

National Museum of African American History and Culture. "Army of the James Medal." https://nmaahc.si.edu/object/nmaahc_2012.37ab.

Oak Alley Foundation. "Dine. Sleep. Explore." Oak Alley Plantation. https://www.oakalleyplantation.org/visit/dine-sleep-explore.

―――. "Slavery Database," Oak Alley Plantation. https://www.oakalleyplantation.org/slavery-database.

Oates, Stephen B. "Children of Darkness," *American Heritage* 26, no. 6 (October, 1973). https://www.americanheritage.com/children-darkness.

Oubre, Claude F. *Forty Acres and a Mule: The Freedmen's Bureau and Black Land Ownership*. Baton Rouge: Louisiana State University Press, 2012, 37.

Philip, M. NourbeSe. *Blank: Essays & Interviews*. Toronto: Book*hug, 2017.

Rasmussen, Daniel. *American Uprising: The Untold Story of America's Largest Slave Revolt*. New York: Harper, 2011.

Satterfield, Stephen. "Our Founding Chefs," *High on the Hog: How African American Cuisine Transformed America*. Season 1, episode 3. Netflix, 2021.

Scott-Heron, Gil. "The Revolution Will Not Be Televised." *Pieces of a Man*. Flying Dutchman Records, 1971.

Sherman, William T. "Special Field Orders, No. 15." Library of Congress. 1865. http://hdl.loc.gov/loc.mss/ms011131.mss83434.256.

Simon, John Y. "The Papers of Ulysses S. Grant, Volume 09: July 7, December 31, 1863." *Volumes of the Papers of Ulysses S. Grant* 1: 195–97. 1982. https://scholarsjunction.msstate.edu/usg-volumes/1/.

Simone, Nina. "Sinnerman." *Pastel Blues*. Philips Records, 1965.

———. "To Be Young, Gifted and Black." *Black Gold*. RCA Victor, 1970.

Snead, James A. "On Repetition in Black Culture." *Black American Literature Forum* 15, no. 4 (1981): 146–54.

Spillers, Hortense J. "Mama's Baby, Papa's Maybe: An American Grammar Book." *Diacritics* 17, no. 2 (1987): 64–81.

Taboclaon, Aleah. "Things to Do in New Orleans: Oak Alley Plantation Tour," Solitary Wanderer, July 16, 2018. https://www.solitarywanderer.com/oak-alley-plantation-tour/.

Truth, Sojourner, and Leslie Podell. "Compare the Speeches," Sojourner Truth Project, 2014. https://www.thesojournertruthproject.com/compare-the-speeches.

Tuskegee Institute Singers. *Go Down Moses*. Victor, 1914.

Virginia Department of Historic Resources. "State Historical Marker 'Blackhead Signpost Road' to Be Dedicated in Southampton County," December 8, 2021. https://www.dhr.virginia.gov/press_releases/state-historical-marker-blackhead-signpost-road-to-be-dedicated-in-southampton-county/.

Visit Edenton. "Visit Edenton, Chowan County, North Carolina." https://www.visitedenton.com/.

Wiencek, Henry. "The Dark Side of Thomas Jefferson," *Smithsonian Magazine*, October 2012. https://www.smithsonianmag.com/history/the-dark-side-of-thomas-jefferson-35976004/.

Wilderson, III, Frank B. *Red, White & Black: Cinema and the Structure of U.S. Antagonisms*. Durham: Duke University Press, 2010.

Wonder, Stevie. "Living for the City." *Innervisions*. Tamla Records, 1973.

Wright, Michelle M. *Physics of Blackness: Beyond the Middle Passage Epistemology*. Minneapolis: University of Minnesota Press, 2015.

Yellin, Jean Fagan. "Written by Herself: Harriet Jacobs' Slave Narrative." *American Literature* 53, no. 3 (1981): 479–86.

Acknowledgements

This work would not exist without the tether of ancestors enslaved in the so-called United States and Jamaica. In these outgrowths of the simple history I was raised with, that was meant to raise a Black man and an American, I look for them and find I can't possibly know them. Looking at my life, I'm certain those ancestors, along with the many enslaved Africans this book is indebted to, would sooner recognize its *mastery* than its subjection. This work was in no small part shaped by that thought. And everything that connects me to them despite it.

Before anything else, I'd like to acknowledge the various internet-accessible governmental, institutional, community-based and solo archive projects, initiatives and resources that made it feasible for me to flit about as I did gathering and dovetailing much of the historical and critical materials that made it into this book. *Bottom Rail on Top* would not have been possible without them, or without the Bibliothèque et Archives nationales du Québec's surprisingly good (and free) JSTOR access. To those on my team, as well as those I butted heads with: I appreciate you.

I'd also like to acknowledge much of the slant and colour at play in "run" was taken from the Nike website in winter 2019. To the multitudes responsible, thank you.

Thank you also to Marcela Huerta and *carte blanche*, who published an early version of "lil chug" under the title "uncle tolliver's tradition." Thank you to the Geopoetics Symposium for the opportunity to present some of this work.

Thank you to Jacquelyn Zong-Li Ross and Deanna Fong at *The Capilano Review* for publishing "new corps." Thank you to Laura Doyle Péan and the Festival de la poésie de Montréal for including my performance of "deus hose" in *Ancrages*, a video project.

Thank you to Canada Council for the Arts, Toronto Arts Council, and Conseil des arts et lettres du Québec for the financial support.

Thank you to Michelle M. Wright, who provided invaluable feedback and encouragement in the middle stages of this work.

Thank you to my editor Cecily Nicholson for the talks, for knowing better, and for so much care.

Thank you to Alayna Munce and Brick Books, as always.

Work like this doesn't make it without someone to insist you really should keep going, and I've been blessed with many such someones. Thank you to Alex Leslie, Ralph Kolewe, River Halen. Thank you to that one not-so-short-lived poetry group. Thank you to Phanuel Antwi for the many long, much-needed phone calls. Thank you to jes dolan for the hungry readership and fresh hell. Thank you to AJ Little, always and forever.

Thank you to Kara Sterne for everything else.

Darby Minott Bradford is a poet and translator based in Tio'tia:ke (Montreal). He is the author of *Dream of No One but Myself* (Brick Books, 2021), which won the A.M. Klein Prize for Poetry, was longlisted for the Grand Prix du livre de Montréal, and was a finalist for the Griffin Poetry Prize, Governor General's Literary Awards, and Gerard Lampert Memorial Award. *House Within a House* by Nicholas Dawson, Bradford's first translation, was published in 2023 by Brick Books. *Bottom Rail on Top* is their second book.